of Aviation

SOPWITH
AVIATION
COMPANY

Early Sopwith aeroplanes, as they appeared in H. Barber's book, *The Aeroplane Speaks*, published in 1916.

Produced in collaboration with

THE *Spirit* OF
BROOKLANDS

Brooklands Museum Trust
Weybridge
Surrey

Tel: 01932 857381

http://www.motor-software.co.uk/brooklands/

IMAGES
of Aviation

SOPWITH
AVIATION
COMPANY

Compiled by
Malcolm Hall

TEMPUS

First published 1999
Copyright © Malcolm Hall, 1999

Tempus Publishing Limited
The Mill, Brimscombe Port,
Stroud, Gloucestershire, GL5 2QG

ISBN 0 7524 1142 X

Typesetting and origination by
Tempus Publishing Limited
Printed in Great Britain by
Midway Clark Printing, Wiltshire

The shop floor at Hoopers, a major Sopwith sub-contractor, when they were building Camels in 1918.

Contents

Introduction		7
1.	The Sportsman Aviator	13
2.	The Aircraft Manufacturer	27
3.	The Dogs of War	43
4.	Sopwiths in Service	77
5.	Atlantic Failure	107
6.	The End – and the Beginning	115
Selected Bibliography and Acknowledgements		128

The Sopwith entry for the first Schneider Trophy contest to be held after the First World War.

Introduction

In one sense, compared to his fellow pioneers of the British aircraft industry, Tommy Sopwith arrived late on the scene. Whilst others such as A. V. Roe, Geoffrey de Havilland and Robert Blackburn were, from the start, intent on designing and building the primitive contraptions in which they hoped eventually to fly, Sopwith, having already acquired a taste for fast cars and motor boats, began his own aviation career by purchasing other men's aeroplanes, with the principal object of taking part in this new sport of flying.

Thomas Octave Murdoch Sopwith was born on 18 January 1888, the son and grandson of engineers. His was a happy and well-off family background (although, when he was only ten, his father died in particularly tragic circumstances) and Tom, as the youngest and only boy, surrounded by seven elder sisters, probably had more than the average share of female love and attention. As he grew older he followed the direction taken by his forebears by attending the Seafield Park Engineering School.

Like other young men of that time, he was attracted to many of the new toys which the young twentieth century was producing and, if they went fast – so much the better! With the resources left him in his father's will, he was able to experience some of these delights. Motorcycles, cars, motorboats, balloons – all were grist to his mill. Aiding him in these pursuits by that time was his erstwhile mechanic, Fred Sigrist, whose own career was to soar in the wake of the Sopwith slipstream. By 1907, when practical aeroplane flying in England was still non-existent, Sopwith had already acquired some experience of the navigation of the skies, being then part-owner with a certain Philip Paddon of a balloon, which they had baptised, without troubling to be unduly imaginative, 'Padsop' and in which he had made a number of flights.

In 1910, however, British aviation was at last beginning to catch up and it was on 18 September that year that, having arrived in Dover harbour aboard his schooner 'Neva', Tommy Sopwith took himself to Tilmanstone, a few miles to the northward, having heard that the American pilot, John B. Moisant, who had just made the first crossing of the Channel carrying a passenger, was at that moment reposing in a field thereabouts, with his Bleriot monoplane. That was the start of it. After making the appropriate enquiries, Sopwith visited the designer and constructor Howard Wright in London and purchased from him an aeroplane – a monoplane like the Bleriot. This he took to Brooklands, Surrey, where many like-minded young men gravitated, with its banked track for the fast-car enthusiasts and the landing ground within it for the use of the intrepid aviators.

There, Sopwith, without benefit of dual instruction, proceeded to see if he could fly his new acquisition. This he managed to do, although not without the discovery that controlling a flimsy aeroplane tended to demand a certain delicacy when manipulating the controls. Soon, the monoplane was lying in one of the Brooklands hangars, very much the worse for wear and awaiting repairs, while its owner, happily, nursed nothing more than a bruise or two. Not to be put off and keen to resume his intriguing encounter with the mysteries of aerodynamics, he purchased a second machine – a biplane this time. His education continued successfully and it was in the latter aeroplane that on 21 November he performed the three flights necessary to satisfy the Royal Aero Club's examiners and was granted his pilot's certificate.

He was now in the air at every opportunity. At the same time, in common with other pioneer aviators of the day, he started to take an interest in the various records and prizes which were waiting to be attacked and claimed. Within weeks, flying around a closed circuit at Brooklands, he had captured the British endurance and distance records. On 18 December, he capped this with an even longer flight, landing in Belgium after nearly four hours in the air, in turbulent conditions, to win the Baron de Forest prize for the longest flight from England to the Continent. All this a bare three months after his first tentative hops and circuits.

So well-known had he now become, in a Britain which was awakening to an awareness that the era of aviation had well and truly arrived, that he found that he had attracted attention at the very pinnacle of the nation. King George V had expressed a wish to see him fly, so, on 1 February 1911, Sopwith flew the biplane from Brooklands to Windsor Castle, where he landed and was duly presented to the King.

In April, Sopwith sailed for the United States, where he demonstrated his flying ability in another of his acquisitions, a Bleriot monoplane, as well as in the Howard Wright biplane, both of which he had shipped across from England. The Bleriot was soon wrecked in one of his not infrequent crashes and was sent back to France for repair. In due course he was joined in America by that other pioneer aviator, the flamboyant Claude Grahame-White, and the next few months saw them both following a busy schedule, giving innumerable passenger flights and taking part in flying meetings and competitions from Philadelphia to Columbus Ohio, in which the British pair carried all before them. Off Manhattan, the Howard Wright went the way of all flesh when it ditched in the sea and it, too, was wrecked.

By October, Sopwith was back in England, still flying other men's aeroplanes, sometimes as a test pilot, and sometimes taking up passengers for their first experience of this novel thrill of flying with the birds. The next step saw his airborne companions becoming more than mere passengers, for in February 1912 he opened his own flying school at Brooklands. Among the pupils who gained their wings was a young Australian who, although destined himself to leave the scene tragically early, contributed a name which was to become for ever widely renowned throughout the aviation world. Harry George Hawker, with his friend and fellow-engineer, Harry Kauper, had arrived in England in May 1911. A year later they were both at Brooklands working 'on the bench'. Within months

Tommy Sopwith in the Martin and Handasyde monoplane which he flew for a period in 1912.

Hawker had persuaded Tommy Sopwith to allow him to learn to fly. The team found that it had acquired another valuable member – one who was to make his mark, not only in the workshop, but also in the design office and, predominantly, in the air.

By this time, Sopwith had made the momentous decision to relinquish the field of flying instruction and to concentrate his energies, once and for all, on the design and construction of his own machines. Tommy Sopwith, the sportsman aviator, had completed his metamorphosis into Mr T.O.M. Sopwith, aeroplane manufacturer.

The first aircraft which could truly claim the Sopwith name made its maiden flight in July 1912 and is usually referred to as the Sopwith-Wright, since it incorporated wings of Wright form. It was a tractor biplane, powered by a 70hp Gnôme engine, and performed well enough to be the subject of a purchase by the Admiralty in order to join the other machines then equipping the Naval Wing of the newly-formed Royal Flying Corps (RFC) at Eastchurch. A second machine was later built; this too joined the Navy and from these two 'first stabs' a succession of roughly similar designs emerged in the next two years.

So far, all the work had been carried out in the Sopwith sheds at Brooklands. As the activities (and the workforce) expanded, larger premises became a requirement, so, towards the end of 1912, these were found a few miles away, in the shape of a roller-skating rink at Kingston-on-Thames. Early in the New Year, another milestone was passed when the Sopwith Aviation Company was registered. The payroll at that time was numbered as twenty-one.

As that crowded year of 1913 ran its course, the little enterprise surged on: a new three-seater aeroplane appeared, owing something to the Sopwith-Wright and powered by an 80hp Gnôme. At the same time, Sopwiths broke new ground (or rather, water) with the first successful British flying boat, a handsome craft which was named the Bat Boat. This first machine was quickly wrecked by a strong wind when it was left untended overnight at Cowes, but a number more were built and sold. Several more three-seaters were produced, while another new biplane made its first appearance. A neat little aeroplane, it was also fitted with an 80hp Gnôme and faster than anything else then in England. Unofficially dubbed the Tabloid, it was the begetter of a high-class pedigree, destined to reach its apogee with the advent of the Camel in 1917. Meanwhile, Harry Hawker had been making his mark. Having proved himself a competent pilot, he turned his attention to record-breaking, while still taking a leading part in both the workshops and the design office.

Three of the tractor biplanes had been fitted with floats and a 100hp Anzani engine; these were also sold to the Admiralty. A fourth, of a broadly similar configuration, was also produced and was entered by Sopwith in a contest for a £5000 prize offered by the *Daily Mail* for a flight completely around these islands – the Circuit of Britain Race. Inevitably, Hawker was the pilot. When all other competitors withdrew, the race seemed in Sopwiths' pocket. However, after completing over 1000 miles of the course, the machine was badly damaged during an attempted landing on the sea near Dublin and the competition was abandoned for that year.

So dawned the fateful year of 1914. Before the shots were fired at Sarajevo, before the statesmen exchanged their uncompromising notes and the armies of Europe clashed at Tannenberg in the east and on the fields of France in the west, much more was to be achieved in the name of Sopwith. In January, Hawker took the first Tabloid home to Australia, where he demonstrated it to his fellow Australians amid scenes of great enthusiasm. In March, Sopwiths was floated as a limited company. In April, at Monte Carlo, a Tabloid seaplane, flown by Howard Pixton, beat the hitherto confident French to win the Schneider Trophy, at an average speed of 85.5mph. More Tabloids were rolling off what had now become the Kingston production line, for delivery to both the Army and the Navy, while, for the latter, a range of floatplanes was also being produced. The little company was expanding rapidly: more land was acquired further down Canbury Park Road, where new workshops were built and staffed with additional workers.

By August another new seaplane was being prepared for that year's Circuit of Britain competition, which was due to start in the middle of the month. By 4 August, it found itself superseded by a sterner contest, as the armies mobilised, marched and fought. As the British Expeditionary Force prepared to embark for France, the RFC took steps to accompany it, while the Royal Naval Air Service (RNAS), as the Naval Wing had become, made its own provisions to support the war at sea. All available aircraft, including the Circuit seaplane, together with the Tabloids and the earlier Tractor biplanes, were pressed into the King's service.

The sudden realities of modern war found all concerned unprepared. The learning was harsh but instructive. While the small British Army fell back from Mons and Le Cateau, above it the RFC's aeroplanes, including several Tabloids, gave valuable service as the Generals' new airborne cavalry, bringing back reports of the whereabouts of the enemy in the chaos of the general retreat. At the same time, on encountering their German counterparts, they began to act as soldiers should, by exchanging pot-shots with pistol or rifle. The Generals, for their part, were beginning to appreciate this new, if somewhat problematical means they had been given of seeing what was going on 'on the other side of the hill'.

In the hands of the RNAS, too, the Tabloid showed its mettle. From a forward base at Antwerp, several examples were involved in the earliest bombing raids of the war, the most successful being that which took place on 9 October, when Flight Lieutenant Marix flew a Tabloid to Düsseldorf and put his bombs straight through the roof of the Zeppelin hangar there, destroying the airship inside.

At Kingston, new versions of the little machine were being devised. Harking back to that spring day at Monte Carlo, it was being turned out as a floatplane, numbers of which were acquired by the RNAS where, perhaps inevitably, they were christened 'Schneider'. These aircraft were embarked in various warships which had been modified to receive them, as the gestation of the aircraft carrier got under way. An improved, re-engined Schneider was next to appear, named the 'Baby'. Several hundreds of these aircraft were built, Sopwiths being obliged, as demand increased, to sub-contract much of the production to Fairey, Blackburn and Parnall.

Nevertheless, in the rough and tumble of wartime conditions, fundamental defects were being uncovered. The nimble Tabloid had been conceived in peacetime, when flying was yet largely a sport, and it was less than adequately robust to survive the rough handling inevitable in the field, while the Schneiders and the other floatplanes were vulnerable to damage in rough seas. Though the Babies saw much service, particularly in the Mediterranean, on the Western Front, Sopwiths were, for a while, a rare breed.

A Schneider ready for launching at the edge of the Thames. The proximity of this water runway made it very useful for flight testing the many floatplanes being turned out at that time.

It was 1916 before the first Sopwith aircraft emerged which was to have a major influence on the war in the air on the British side. It was a two-seater, designated the Type 9400, but soon to be universally dubbed the $1\frac{1}{2}$ Strutter, by reason of the arrangement of its wing bracing structure. It was also the first Sopwith machine to possess what would become an accepted, indeed essential offensive feature – a machine gun mounted in front of the pilot and firing by an interrupter gear through the propeller disc. It was soon followed by its single-seater cousin, the Type 9901, which, as the Pup, collected its own *nom de guerre*. To complete a trio of excellent fighting machines, Sopwiths produced the Triplane. The company had now well and truly arrived as one of the leading producers of fighting aircraft of the war. Yet the best was still to come.

When, in May 1916, the first squadrons were equipped with the $1\frac{1}{2}$ Strutter, its quality was such that it was considered well able to look after itself in the face of the enemy machines then in the sky. By April 1917, however – Bloody April in the annals of the RFC – casualties before the guns of the Albatros D.III and the Fokker Triplane were reaching alarming proportions and the $1\frac{1}{2}$ Strutter was not spared. The standards of aircraft design had moved further on and the RFC desperately needed improved fighting aircraft. It had to wait until the summer, then they came in a rush – the Bristol Fighter, the Royal Aircraft Factory's SE5a and, not least, the Sopwith Camel. In fact, it was the Royal Navy which, having been first with its contract, was the first to receive Camels, delivered to No.4 (Naval) Squadron in June 1917. The RFC's 70 Squadron exchanged its Strutters for Camels a month later. As other units were also re-equipped, the Camel's outstanding maneouvrability made it, in the hands of experienced pilots, a potent factor in the regaining of Allied air supremacy and, statistically, the most successful fighter. In the end, it had shot down more enemy aircraft than any other on either side.

While the Camel was helping to gain the upper hand over the *Jagdstaffeln*, the design office at Kingston was far from idle. Four more types were to be designed and produced in quantity before the Armistice was declared.

The Cuckoo was a torpedo-bomber which, with Sopwiths heavily committed on other work, was partially developed and manufactured in quantity by Blackburns. It was embarked in the Navy's early aircraft carriers, although too late to become involved in hostilities.

The $1\frac{1}{2}$ Strutter. The constructors of this machine, Mann, Egerton & Co., were another of the Sopwith sub-contractors.

The Dolphin was a single-seat fighter, like the Camel, but without the latter's compact appearance. It was, for the time, very heavily armed, having two synchronised Vickers *à la* Camel, as well as two Lewises firing over the top plane.

The Snipe and the Salamander were similar in general design and both, in their general lines, more obviously related to the Camel than was the Dolphin. The Snipe was designed as the Camel replacement and arrived in France in September 1918, in time to score a number of successes in the last months of the war. The Salamander was the last to emerge and was designed specifically for a new role – that of trench fighter or, as it would now be termed, ground-attack aircraft. However, it was destined not to reach squadron service as, with unexpected suddenness, hostilities came to an end and the noisy anvils of war fell silent. The world, which had been clamouring for armaments for four years, was more than glad to turn its back on such things. Contracts had been placed for 1400 Salamanders. Of these, 1200 were cancelled.

With orders from the fighting services all but non-existent, the company struggled on through the difficult days of 1919. New designs were not lacking, as the team strained to attract sales in both the military and civilian fields. Inevitably, given the situation, there were a number of 'one-offs' which found no market: Snark, Snapper and Cobham were but three. One example, however, was to occupy a special niche in aviation history. With the coming of peace, the *Daily Mail* prize of 1913 for the first non-stop crossing of the Atlantic was renewed and, in 1919, a version of the B1 bomber was prepared for the attempt. That it failed did not detract from the endeavour, the courage and the airmanship which informed the project, while the dramatic circumstances which attended the fate of the pilot and navigator, lost amid the Atlantic wastes, caught the imagination of the nation.

In the end, in September 1920, the decision was taken to wind up the company, while its creditors could still be paid 'twenty shillings in the pound'. The observance of this admirable precept found its reward with the great success enjoyed by its successor the Hawker Company, launched two months later, as in the years that followed, aviation evolved and soared to heights undreamt of in those early years of youthful endeavour inside the Brooklands racing track.

Another scene at the Sopwith sub-contractor Hoopers, with the workforce assembled around a Camel ready for delivery.

One
The Sportsman Aviator

At the time when Louis Bleriot made the first airborne crossing of the English Channel, on 25 July 1909, only a handful of men in Great Britain were managing to coax their machines (mostly French-built) off the ground. A year later, the scene had changed considerably. Men such as A.V. Roe and Samuel Cody were flying their own designs and much aerial activity was to be seen at the newly established aerodromes of Brooklands and Eastchurch. Thus, if Tommy Sopwith had not gone to see Moisant and his Bleriot in that Kentish field in September 1910, he would surely have encountered some other trigger to fire his aeronautical ambitions. Once the aircraft bug had bitten, there was no antidote. Following his encounter with Moisant, Sopwith took himself immediately to Brooklands, where Mrs Maurice Hewlett, the second woman in Britain to fly solo and the first to acquire a pilot's certificate, had her own Henri Farman aircraft. For the sum of £5, the young sportsman was flown around the aerodrome circuit by Mrs Hewlett's pilot, the Frenchman Gustav Blondeau. The next steps followed swiftly: first, an Avis monoplane and then a biplane, both built by Howard Wright, were purchased and taken to Brooklands. Thus equipped, Sopwith set himself to learn to fly and soon found himself a leading member of the small band of young enthusiasts exploring this new and sometimes dangerous pursuit. When he felt himself to be a competent pilot (with many fewer hours as 'pilot in command' than would be thought appropriate today!), he progressed by stages, seemingly not altogether planned, to his ultimate destination. After the American adventure, when he accrued both flying experience and prize money, he spent a little while as a test pilot, while continuing to fly his own machines, now four in number, and introducing numerous daring passengers to the 'sport of flying'. This was followed by the opening in February 1912 of the Sopwith School of Flying, to be exchanged, in less than a year, for the young engineer-pilot's ultimate destiny – the first Sopwith-designed aeroplane had flown and the 'Sopwith Aviation Company' was a going concern.

Tommy Sopwith teaching himself to fly his Avis Monoplane (40hp E.N.V. engine). His very first sortie ended in misfortune; in trying to control his height, he overcorrected, as all learner pilots are wont to do, and his £630 aeroplane was soon lying in a hangar, awaiting repair.

Once Sopwith had acquired his second aircraft, the 60hp Howard Wright biplane, and had gained his RAeC pilot's certificate, he lost no time in imprinting his mark upon the British aviation scene. First, on 10 November 1910, he made his bid for the British Empire Michelin Cup, offered for the longest flight in that current year. Flying around a closed circuit at Brooklands, he recorded a total distance of 107 ¾ miles, thus beating the previous best by Samuel Cody of 95 miles. This done, the young pilot, with all of two month's piloting experience behind him, identified his next goal. This was the Baron de Forest prize of £4000 for the longest flight from England to any point on the Continent, again before the end of the year. Having made Fred Sigrist fit a larger fuel tank (shown above), he set off from Eastchurch on 18 December in seasonally poor visibility and gusty conditions. When he landed, three and a half hours later, forced down by the inclement weather rather than lack of fuel, he found himself near Beaumont, some forty miles south of Brussels, and 177 miles from his point of departure.

A general view of the Howard-Wright, with Sopwith at the controls.

The future captain of industry and present daring aviator of those days was clearly not averse to donning creased overalls and getting his hands dirty.

By the time Sopwith, accompanied by his sister May, had sailed for the United States, he had acquired a third machine – a Bleriot XI monoplane this time, powered by a 70hp Gnôme engine. The Howard-Wright was also shipped out but, not content with these, he also bought during his stay a fourth aeroplane – the Burgess-Wright shown above, with its owner at the controls. The six months he spent in America were packed with activity and incident: in friendly competition with Grahame-White, Sopwith took his mounts to numerous aviation meetings and exhibitions in different States; many members of the public were given their first taste of flying; there were competitions, races, interviews with the Press, the occasional stunt and one or two crashes.

One day while Sopwith was in America, the liner *Olympic*, sister ship to the *Titanic*, sailed from New York to return to Europe after her maiden voyage in the opposite direction, a year before her ill-fated sister. It was proposed that the 'intrepid birdman' should fly out and drop a package on the liner's deck. Sopwith duly set off in the Howard Wright, arriving over the ship as she sailed by Staten Island, causing much excitement on board. Some thirty years later, the release of objects from a moving aircraft, with the intention of hitting a point on the earth's surface below, was still causing the men of Bomber Command, with the benefit of devices such as Oboe, Gee and H2S, a deal of trouble. That day, with no means of refining his aim, Sopwith was in much worse case. He missed.

Tommy Sopwith in his Martinsyde Type 4B, which he purchased after his return from America.

T.O.M. Sopwith, equipped for cold weather flying (certainly on the hands at any rate!).

Of Thomas' seven sisters, May was the one who was usually on hand and in support during his early exploits. Here, she and her brother pose, begoggled, in his monoplane.

After his return from America, Sopwith widened his experience still further, by acting as test pilot of this biplane (100hp Gnôme), built by the Coventry Ordnance Works. It was entered in the Military Aeroplane Trials of 1912 at Larkhill, but hardly flew and came nowhere.

The second Coventry Ordnance machine entered in the Military Trials sported a most elegant rudder but was an even greater disappointment than the first. Fitted with a 110hp Chenu engine, it seems not to have left the ground at all at Larkhill, much, no doubt, to Tommy Sopwith's frustration.

The SOPWITH SCHOOL of Flying.

BROOKLANDS, WEYBRIDGE)

4 ENTIRELY DIFFERENT TYPES of AEROPLANES

American Wright
Howard Wright } BIPLANES (with dual control)

Blériot
Howard Wright } MONOPLANES

— TUITION ON ANY TYPE —

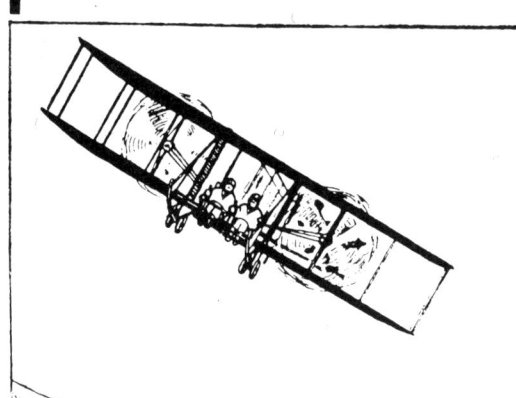

£75
(Including all Breakages and Third Party Risks)

Special Terms to Officers of either Service.

For further information apply to The

Sopwith Aviation School
Brooklands, Weybridge, Surrey.

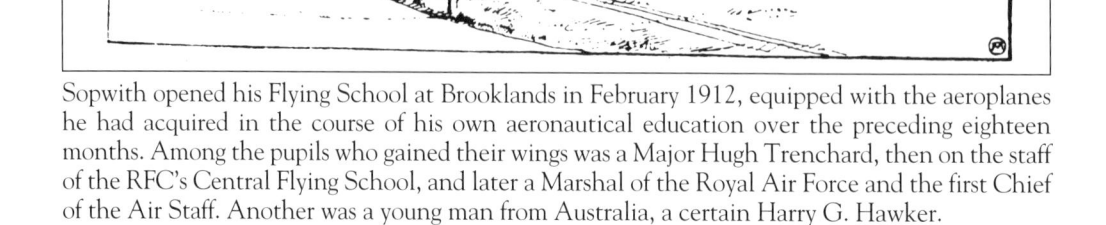

Sopwith opened his Flying School at Brooklands in February 1912, equipped with the aeroplanes he had acquired in the course of his own aeronautical education over the preceding eighteen months. Among the pupils who gained their wings was a Major Hugh Trenchard, then on the staff of the RFC's Central Flying School, and later a Marshal of the Royal Air Force and the first Chief of the Air Staff. Another was a young man from Australia, a certain Harry G. Hawker.

The next move was a watershed: the little band, led by Sopwith and Sigrist, built its own machine. A new fuselage, housing a 70hp Gnôme, was married to wings copied from the Burgess-Wright, hence its usual appellation of 'Sopwith-Wright', the first flight taking place on 4 July 1912. The lady in attendance must surely be Sopwith's sister, May.

The Sopwith-Wright (sometimes also referred to as the 'hybrid') in flight. Several more years were to elapse before it became established practice to confer on an aircraft type an official name.

The following stage in the evolution of the Sopwith family of aircraft is usually referred to as the Three-Seater Tractor Biplane. With this, Sopwiths can be said to have arrived as a manufacturing concern: a number were built and sold to both the Navy and the Army.

One of Sopwith's Three-Seater Tractor Biplanes in the hands of the Army, on Salisbury Plain.

By now, the enterprise had outgrown the accommodation at Brooklands and, just before Christmas 1912, the 'Central Hall' roller-skating rink in Canbury Park Road, Kingston-upon-Thames was acquired. On the right: the rink's 'Buttons', Jack Whitehorn, who 'came with the premises' and was to become the longest-serving employee of the Sopwith and Hawker companies.

On the very day that Sopwith sold his first aircraft to the Admiralty, he engaged his first draughtsman, one R.J. Ashfield, a local teacher (though not at the Tiffin School, as used to be thought). This small hut, built on the roof of the rink, was his original DO.

A new departure, during the same period, was represented by the first 'Bat Boat', the hull of which was made at Cowes by the yacht builder, Sam Saunders. Fitted with a 90hp Austro-Daimler engine, it was exhibited at Olympia in February and then taken to Cowes for testing. The first attempts to get the Bat Boat to fly were unsuccessful. This failure was joined by misfortune when the machine, having been drawn up on the beach for the night, was found wrecked in the morning, overturned by a strong wind. The forward elevator, seen here, was later removed, as in the lower photograph.

After repair, the Bat Boat was successfully flown. Then, in July 1913, powered by a 100hp Green and fitted with manually retractable wheels (referred to at the time as a 'Folding Landing Chassis'), it entered the Mortimer Singer competition. This competition was offered for a British amphibian which could demonstrate its ability to land and take off from both land and water. There being no other serious competitors, in the hands of Harry Hawker it duly carried off the prize of £500 and notched up another success for the now-famous Sopwith stable.

In 1914, further Bat Boats were built, like those shown here at Cowes, fitted with 200hp Canton-Unné engines and with the upper wing span extended by another fourteen feet. Both types of Bat Boat were sold to the Admiralty. In addition – and it is intriguing to contemplate the fact – with war against Germany only months away, one of these aircraft was even supplied to that country.

THE SOPWITH AVIATION CO.

CONTRACTORS TO THE ADMIRALTY.

RECORDS

British Duration Record	8 hrs. 23 mins.
British Height Record (Pilot alone)	11,450 ft.
British Height Record (Pilot & 1 Passenger)	12,900 ft.
British Height Record (Pilot & 2 Passengers)	10,600 ft.
WORLD'S Height Record (Pilot & 3 Passengers)	8,400 ft.

Winner of the Mortimer-Singer Competition for the first all-British machine to rise from and alight on LAND and WATER.

Offices and Works:
KINGSTON-ON-THAMES

Telephone:
1777 KINGSTON

Telegrams:
"SOPWITH KINGSTON"

By now, the company was able to boast a number of records, which did no harm to its growing reputation.

Two
The Aircraft Manufacturer

By 1913, aviation was involved in two quite distinct sectors of the nation's activities. For their part, the military men had begun to comprehend that the presence of flying machines would bring fundamental changes to the battlefield. They would be of a wider dimension than those already conferred by the tethered balloon and advantages would accrue to the general who had access to an effective air corps. By contrast, for the general public flocking every weekend to the new airfields like Hendon and Brooklands, aviation was very much an entertainment of the sporting kind, where the now-famous pilots such as Hawker, Pégoud, Hamel or Hucks could be watched performing 'stunts' or banking steeply around the pylons marking a racecourse which, in those days, could easily be contained within the aerodrome and thus the spectators' view. As aspiring manufacturers, Sopwiths were, of course, involved with both these sectors. Success in the sporting field was good for business and aircraft bearing the Sopwith name were usually to be found in the lists of contestants, while, as we have already seen, both the War Office and the Admiralty had Sopwith aircraft on charge.

When, in 1913, the Daily Mail offered a £5000 prize for the winner of a race around the British Isles by seaplanes, Sopwith, inevitably, figured on the list of entries. In the event, the Sopwith seaplane (100hp Green) was the only starter. Crewed by the two Australian Harries, Hawker and Kauper, it took off from the Solent at 5.30 a.m. on 25 August and by the afternoon had reached Scarborough.

During its short stay, it naturally became an object of great interest to the Scarborough holidaymakers. At the end of the next day, it found itself at Oban, on the West coast. By this time, over 800 miles of the 1500-mile 'Circuit' had been covered.

It was on the third day that disaster struck: In attempting to land on the sea just off the coast near Dublin for a minor adjustment, Hawker side-slipped into the water and the aircraft was wrecked. The aircraft was recovered from the sea and that was the end of any attempt on the prize.

The little Tabloid (wingspan 25ft 6in) came as a revelation. Powered by the ubiquitous 80hp Gnôme, it demonstrated a top speed of 92mph. The lower photograph was taken at Hendon on 29 November 1913, when Harry Hawker showed off its abilities in front of a large and appreciative Saturday crowd. In early Tabloids, the wide cockpit accommodated the pilot and a passenger side by side. The name 'Tabloid' excited a certain protestation from the pharmaceutical firm of Burroughs Wellcome, who considered it their copyright, which had thus been infringed. However, the name had been conferred quite unofficially and not by Sopwith's themselves, who were thus innocent of any offence and no legal action ensued. It may well be that the fame which the aircraft subsequently earned represented publicity which turned out to be useful to the pill-makers as well!

Harry Hawker at Hendon. The young Australian had become a popular and celebrated national figure.

One of the first Tabloids taking off from Brooklands. After the first batch, the looming needs of war resulted in orders from both the Admiralty and the War Office and these later machines were built as single-seaters.

Derived from the Tabloid, this was a one-off aeroplane variously dubbed the Sociable, the Tweenie or the Churchill. It was larger all round than its progenitor and seems to have been intended as a trainer, since it returned to the original Tabloid two-seater arrangement and was fitted with dual controls.

In January 1914, accompanied by the first Tabloid, Hawker and Kauper sailed for Australia. After demonstration flights at Melbourne, they went on to several other locations, including Sydney, where the aircraft was flown from Randwick Racecourse (above) and where many people were given flights, including the Governor General, Lord Denman.

Caulfield Racecourse, Victoria, was also converted to a temporary airfield. There, the enthusiastic crowds became something of a hazard, encroaching on the flying area to such an extent that Hawker sometimes found it difficult to land and take off with safety.

The two Harries returned from Australia in June, with the precious Tabloid, pictured above with Sopwith and Hawker standing by the nose.

After the acquisition of the ex-skating rink, further floor space soon became necessary to the growing company, so the company expanded into this building further down Canbury Park Road.

Meanwhile back inside the skating rink, the workforce pauses from its work on the Tabloid assembly line and around a gleaming Bat Boat hull, to have their pictures taken.

The first Schneider Trophy contest was held in 1913, when there were no entries from Great Britain. By the next year, however, the Tabloid had flown and was in production. With Hawker and the first aircraft in Australia, another Tabloid was fitted with floats and a 100hp Monosoupape Gnôme and dispatched to Monte Carlo for the race, accompanied by Howard Pixton, who had been engaged as test pilot in Hawker's absence. Although there had been some trouble with the float configuration back home and the pilot had very little experience on the type, on the day (20 April) all went like clockwork. The two French pilots had expected to have things all their own way, but to their consternation they found themselves overhauled by the hitherto despised British entry. One by one, they and the other competitors dropped out, until Pixton found himself lapping the course alone, signalling the end of French dominance of European aviation.

A close-up of the triumphant Tabloid at Monte Carlo, floats well awash.

Howard Pixton talking to Jacques Schneider (on the right), after the race. Pixton was offered champagne in celebration, but confessed himself (*ah, les anglais!*) more partial to a glass of Bass.

The Gordon Bennett racer was another Tabloid variant. With a much slimmer fuselage and a reshaped tail unit, it was intended for the Gordon Bennett Aviation Cup of 1914. War came first and, given the number 1215, it joined the other aircraft which were called up by the RNAS.

The 1914 Circuit of Britain (planned for August) was another competition which found itself cancelled by the outbreak of war. The Sopwith entry was to be the machine above, initially fitted with a wheeled undercarriage as shown. It never got as far as the fitment of floats, but was the inspiration for two other Sopwith types. One was the Two-Seater Scout (opposite), twenty-four of which were built and supplied to the RNAS.

A Two-Seater Scout at the RNAS Station, Great Yarmouth. The type cannot have been too popular, since it became generally known as the Spinning Jenny – for this is what it apparently did, at a time when, for many pilots, the spin was still a mysterious and frightening phenomenon.

The type 807 seaplane was built to an Admiralty specification and was the other derivation from the 1914 Circuit of Britain aircraft. It embodied folding wings – a feature already patented by the Short brothers for their own floatplanes. An amicable arrangement was reached, with the payment by Sopwith of a modest royalty of £15. All the last three types illustrated were fitted with the 100hp Monosoupape Gnôme.

By 1913, the scent of war was growing stronger in Europe's chancelleries. Inevitably, increasing thought was given in certain more enlightened quarters to the uses to which the aeroplane could be put in battle. In the naval sphere, one application which was discerned was the launching from it of a torpedo. Sopwith, building on their experience with their other seaplanes, designed the Type C in order to explore this new field. To lift into the air and deliver a 14in torpedo weighing as much as 900lb, necessarily demanded a much larger machine than its predecessors. This, the Type C undoubtedly was, while a 200hp Canton-Unné provided the greater power deemed to be necessary. Only one was built, but it led to the design and construction of the Type 860, powered by a 225hp Sunbeam and which is the aircraft pictured above.

Eighteen Type 860s were built, at least some of which saw service in the Mediterranean, including the Gallipoli campaign in 1915. When put to the test at that time, these early machines encountered difficulty in rising from the water with their heavy warloads and achieved little of note.

A Type 860 at Great Yarmouth in August 1915.

In 1913-1914, another series of 'pusher' aircraft was produced, quite different from the more handsome Bat Boat. The 'Gun Bus' (above), fitted with a 150hp Sunbeam engine, represented the land-plane version.

The seaplane version (100hp Anzani) is generally known as the 'Greek Seaplane', since it was originally produced to fulfil an order from the Greek government.

Three
The Dogs of War

By the time that the cannons began to roar, Sopwith, in common with other aircraft manufacturers such as Shorts and Avro, had in a very brief time become established as contractors for the supply of warplanes to both the Admiralty and the War Office. For more than a year, this largely meant the Tabloid and its progeny, the Schneider and the Baby. With the arrival of the 1½ Strutter and the Pup however, a new standard was established. These were aeroplanes designed for war from the outset. But, if they were a step forward, the Triplane was a stride and the Camel, in 1917, was a leap. In 1912-1913, the Sopwith output amounted to only some twenty-odd aeroplanes. During the four wartime years, a total of 16,000 aircraft were turned out, if those from the sub-contractors are included, while, as the war in the air evolved and as the designers found new inspirations, more new types came tumbling out. From the Cuckoo to the Snipe, from the Dolphin to the Salamander, something like a dozen distinct new types emerged during the last eighteen months of hostilities. To cope with all this, an entirely new factory had been built at Ham, on the outskirts of Kingston, with a vast floor area needed to contain the rows of aircraft being assembled to feed the ravenous war machine. When at last the fighting stopped, all the hectic activity of the previous four years stopped too. Clearly, as the statesmen sat at Versailles and planned the peace, there was going to be no requirement for all those fighting aircraft which had so recently been demanded in such great numbers. Future hopes must bend more towards civil aviation, but what forms would that unknown world assume?

This scene in the skating rink one year after the outbreak of war reveals a well-filled production line of Schneiders.

A completed Schneider (serial number 3739) inside the skating rink, on its launching trolley and ready for towing the short distance from Canbury Park Road through Kingston town to the river.

Another Schneider, outside and packed on its road transport in 1915. Sopwiths were now very much 'On His Majesty's Service'!

The first three pusher seaplanes were delivered to Greece, where they saw effective service as training aircraft with the Royal Hellenic Navy. However, when war broke out, the remaining six of the type were commandeered by the British Admiralty, being given the designation Type 880, while their Anzani engines were replaced with 100hp Gnômes. As can be seen, the nacelles on these aircraft differed markedly from those on the original landplane 'Gun Buses' (compare with the upper photograph on page 42). In the early months of the war, some of the 'Greek' seaplanes found their way to France, their floats having been removed and replaced by wheels. They were not found to be greatly useful and were soon returned to 'Home Establishment'.

Two more Schneiders ready to go. A total of 137 were built, all of them by Sopwiths at Kingston. Most Schneiders had the triangular fins shown, while lateral control was still achieved by wing-warping, as employed by the Wrights. Only a small number of the later machines possessed ailerons and the larger fin of the aircraft in the upper photograph opposite. Embarked in various 'seaplane carriers', and obtained by the conversion of assorted vessels, from tramp steamers to Cross-Channel packets, Schneiders accompanied the Fleet in both the North Sea and the Eastern Mediterranean.

These two Schneiders, having arrived at the riverbank by R.J. Turk's boatyard, are ready for launching. The nearer aircraft is a later model than the ones illustrated previously, as is revealed by its reshaped fin.

The Baby seaplane (above) was an improved Schneider and entered service in late 1915. The early Babies retained their predecessor's 100hp Gnôme, but the majority were re-engined with 110hp Clergets, under a redesigned cowling.

47

Baby seaplanes on the production line. Sopwiths produced exactly 100, but, by 1916, demand for warplanes was beyond the capacity of the parent firm alone and sub-contracting now came into vogue.

The firm chosen was Blackburns, which built the remainder of the Babies, some 186 in all, in their own former skating rink in Leeds. They were then taken by road to Brough, beside the River Humber in East Yorkshire for flight-testing.

Three Schneiders and a Type 807 'Folder', ready to go down the slipway for test flight or delivery.

This Schneider, at the Albany Boat House, was experimentally fitted with floats designed by Major Linton-Hope.

In 1915, as the months went by, the form taken by aerial warfare evolved and became more clear. Lessons were learned and put into effect by the aircraft companies' designers. At Sopwiths, the Type 9400, which appeared at the beginning of 1916 and was soon to be known as the 1½ Strutter, was the first fruit of these latest ideas. It was powered by either a 110hp or a 130hp Clerget rotary engine.

The 'Strutter' adopted what had now become the standard two-seat configuration, with the observer – and his Lewis gun – behind the pilot, while the latter, at last, was given a Vickers, firing through the propeller disc by means of an interrupter gear. That used in the 1½ Strutter was designed by Harry Kauper, that other Australian and clearly no mean engineer, although languishing in Hawker's shadow.

These two views inside the skating rink provide an excellent illustration of the detailed design of the wing ribs and spars, together with the fuselage structure, of a typical Sopwith aircraft.

Hard on the heels of the 1½ Strutter came the 'Pup' (unofficial names still reigned), the prototype of which is pictured above.

Although overshadowed by the Camel, its more glamorous sister, the Pup proved to be a doughty fighting machine, with handling qualities which earned it the admiration of all who flew it. Much used by the RNAS, both on land and at sea, the best part of 2,000 Pups were built, the majority by sub-contractors. Both in France and in the Mediterranean, the Pup was still flying and fighting in 1918.

Contractors to H.M. Government.

WHITEHEAD AIRCRAFT, Ltd.

Works: Richmond, Surrey.   'Phone: Richmond, 1866 (Private Branch Exchange).
Fulham.   'Phone: West, 1663.

Aerodrome: Hanworth Park, Middlesex.   'Phone: Feltham, 6.

Whitehead, conveniently close to Sopwiths, was another aspirant aircraft manufacturer which prospered on sub-contracts. In the case of the Pup, they were the major sub-contractor, building no less than 820 of them.

53

A portion of the Old Works at the Whitehead Aircraft factory.

The 80hp Le Rhône rotary engine was fitted to the Pup scout aircraft. It was one of a range of rotaries, from the 50hp seven-cylinder Gnôme to the nine-cylinder 130hp Clerget and 180hp Le Rhône. Until the third year of the war, if you needed a reliable engine for your scout aircraft, you had virtually no choice but to shop in France.

Last of the 1916 trio which confirmed Sopwiths as the leading British manufacturer of fighting aeroplanes. The Triplane owed much to the Pup structurally, though it benefited from the extra power conferred by a 130hp Clerget and was renowned for its rate of climb. It was used exclusively by the Navy.

View of the Triplane cockpit. The three instruments from left to right are: RPM indicator, compass and airspeed indicator.

As well as the 'standard' Triplane, two more were produced that were slightly larger in size and fitted with Hispano-Suiza engines. That in N510, on the left, was of 200hp with a geared drive to the propeller, while N509, on the right, had a direct-drive 150hp engine.

Early in 1916, the fertile minds in the Sopwith design office hit upon a novel concept, and a strange structure, designated the LRT Tr, began to take shape in the Kingston shops (the engine is a 250hp Rolls-Royce Eagle I). The idea was to persuade a gunner, with a Lewis, to sit in the upper nacelle for the purpose, amongst other things, of shooting down Zeppelins.

When it was complete, the LRT Tr was taken to Brooklands and flown. Some kind thoughts, at least, appear to have been given to the well-being of the upper crew member, the object of the quadricycle undercarriage being to prevent the craft from nosing over on landing. Only one LRT Tr was built and the project was soon abandoned, probably to the relief of any RFC observers who may have got wind of it.

Fred Sigrist in lighthearted conversation with an unknown officer (about the LRT Tr perhaps?). By now, Sigrist had come a long way from the days when he was Tommy Sopwith's chauffeur and marine mechanic.

The Bee was a one-off with a difference. It was knocked up out of spare Pup components and fitted with a 50hp Gnôme to become Harry Hawker's runabout and display aircraft.

And so dawned 1917 and with it the birth of the *Jasta*, bringing German ascendancy in the air and a period when military expediency obliged the RFC to sustain heavy losses in combat with superior German machines. While the airmen suffered, the industry at home was striving to give them some more advanced machines in which to fly and fight. One of these was the F.1 Camel, the first prototype of which is shown above at Brooklands. In June, Camels went into service with the RNAS and with the RFC soon after that. The turning of the tide was at hand.

This F.1 Camel is seen partly assembled at Hooper's of Chelsea, another of the Sopwith subcontractors. The F.1, of which over 5,000 were built, used several different engines, but the majority had 130hp Clerget rotaries.

The 2F.1 Camel, on the other hand, was fitted exclusively with W.O. Bentley's B.R.1 (designated originally the A.R.1) – at last a British rotary engine (and a good one) had become available. Most 2F.1 Camels went to the RNAS for shipboard operations.

The tapered-wing Camel (designation F.1/1) was an experiment in aerodynamic refinement which did not come off, since both performance and manoeuvrability were inferior to the standard design and only the aircraft shown was built.

To a young pilot with only few hours – and those on a docile trainer – the Camel could come as a bit of a handful. A number of Camels were therefore turned into two-seaters, as shown here (B2504 at No. 32 TDS Montrose).

Contemporaneously with the Camel, the engineers at Sopwiths also turned their minds to bomber aircraft. The B.1 was a single-seater like the Camel, but twice as heavy, with a 500lb bomb load and a 200hp Hispano-Suiza to propel it skywards. Although it got as far as being tested under operational conditions, it did not go into service.

The Cuckoo shipborne torpedo bomber possessed great similarities with the B.1, differing by its engine (200hp Sunbeam Arab), folding wings and separate axles to allow the torpedo to be accommodated. After the first prototype had been built by Sopwiths, the whole project, including development and the greater part of the production, was handed over to the Blackburn Aircraft Company.

The first Dolphin prototype made its initial flight on 23 May 1917, needless to say in the hands of Harry Hawker, seen above in a relaxed mood. This was the only Dolphin to be fitted with the frontal radiator shown. In the production aircraft, a radiator was installed on each side of the fuselage.

A production Dolphin I, showing the improved pilot's view conferred by the modified cowling around the 200hp Hispano-Suiza. The view was further refined by the backward staggering of the top wing, which raised eyebrows at the time. The really remarkable feature of the Dolphin, however, was its generous allocation of weapons, with twin Lewises firing upwards and twin Vickers firing through the propeller disc.

The science of ergonomics was still in the future when the Dolphin cockpit was designed – correction: 'happened'. The instrument in the right-hand corner seems to be completely hidden from the pilot's view by the machine gun.

As well as building several hundred Camels, Hooper's received substantial orders for Dolphins. Above, the assembly line arranged with meticulous precision. Below, the workforce is informally paraded as a useful reminder of the unsung stalwarts who kept the fighting squadrons equipped.

While various bellicose machines were being turned out, designed to fly higher and faster while carrying heavier armament for the discomforture of the Hun, the dainty Sparrow, with its two-cylinder 35hp ABC Gnat, comes almost as light relief. However, it was intended that it should be radio-controlled and it seems that it too, had it not been curtailed, might have entered the fray as an early flying bomb!

After the Sparrow, back to reality with the 2B.2 Rhino (230hp BHP), another triplane, another bomber. The first aircraft (X7) flew at Brooklands in October 1917.

The second Rhino, X8, did not make its appearance in the sky until February 1918. It was also the last and the two aircraft were relegated to tasks as flying test beds.

The 3F.2 Hippo was a two-seat fighter, designed in response to a French requirement, to replace their 1½ Strutters. First flight was on 13 September 1917 but, although several more were built, trouble was experienced with both the wings and the engine (a new eleven-cylinder Clerget) and the type never saw service.

Although, at first sight, the 2FR.2 Bulldog would appear to bear a superficial resemblance to the Hippo – and was also designed as a two-seat fighter – it embodied a considerable proportion of original design work. Back-stagger, for one thing, was abandoned, while the crew were housed together in a single cockpit, the view being enhanced by a completely open centre-section. The first Bulldog, which started its trials in November 1917, had the same engine as the Hippo, though this was replaced in the second aircraft (illustrated above) by a 360hp ABC Dragonfly radial. By that time, another fundamental change had been wrought in the design, in that the original single-bay wing structure had become two-bay, as shown, and no less than eight feet had been added to the span. As with the Rhino, this second machine was the last of its line and the two Bulldogs ended their lives on general experimental work.

Amidst all the drawing office activity which had produced some six or seven separate types in quick succession, three more distinct designs were taking shape on the drawing boards, two of which were to see quantity production. The first of these, making its appearance in late 1917, was the 7F.1 Snipe, powered by W.O. Bentley's B.R.2 rotary, developing 230hp. It entered service later on in 1918, with the objective of replacing the Camels in the squadrons.

A view of the installation of the Snipe's twin Vickers. Instruments still jostling with guns!

That some thirty-seven persons could be gathered for this photograph, yet constitute no more than the Kingston Inspection staff, is one measure of how much the company had expanded during the four years of the War. In fact, by the Armistice, the total payroll had risen to 3,500.

The carpenters' shop at Ham.

The 8F.1 Snail marked an interesting step in the evolution of aircraft structural design. The first Snail, C4284, was conventional enough, but in answer to an official request, C4288, shown above, featured a first attempt at monocoque or stressed-skin construction, with the fuselage covering formed of load-bearing plywood. The Snail was also asked to bear the burden of marriage with a new form of powerplant – the ABC Wasp radial engine. Teething troubles ensued and no more Snails were built.

The cockpit of C4284, seen through the centre-section cut-out (not embodied in the second machine).

By early 1918, the RFC was being called upon to devote more and more effort to ground attack work, to assist the army in its trench warfare. At first it seemed a good idea to mount two Lewis guns, firing downwards through the cockpit floor, thus creating the TF.1 Camel, as shown.

Only one TF.1 was produced, it being then decided to do the job properly by the design of a completely new aircraft – the TF.2 Salamander, the prototype of which, E5429, made its first flight at Brooklands on 27 April 1918. With its 230hp Bentley B.R.2, it owed more to the Snipe than to the Camel.

71

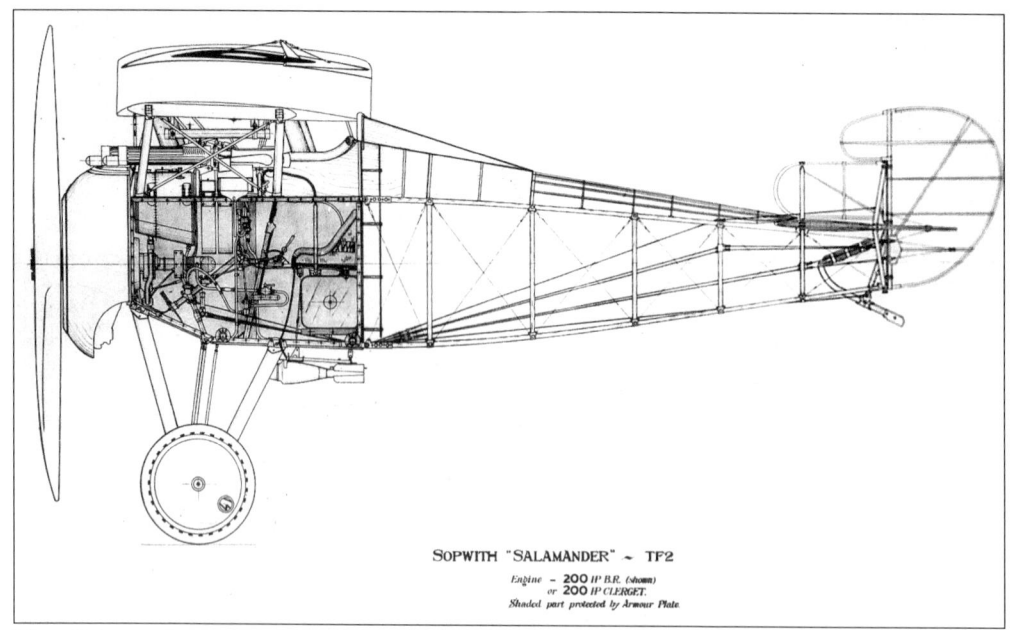

SOPWITH "SALAMANDER" - TF2
Engine - 200 IP B.R. (shown)
or 200 IP CLERGET.
Shaded part protected by Armour Plate.

This Salamander drawing not only shows details of the structural design, it also provides a general indication, by the shaded area, of where armoured plating was incorporated to protect the pilot from ground fire, which was responsible for a high proportion of the casualties being incurred. At the same time, the downward firing Lewises of the TF.1 were rejected in favour of the standard twin Vickers in front of the pilot.

A production Salamander, one of 163 built by Sopwiths. Of a total of 1,406 Salamanders originally ordered (mostly from sub-contractors), over 1,200 were summarily cancelled, not on account of some major failure of design, but due to the outbreak of peace. The type never reached the squadrons and can perhaps stand as an outstanding but by no means solitary example of the nearly mortal blow which the ending of hostilities dealt to the young British aircraft industry.

In April 1918, an early Snipe, B9967, was modified to take a 360hp ABC Dragonfly radial engine in order to give the type the higher performance that the new engine promised. It was taken to Brooklands and first tested on 27 April, on the same day that the first Salamander made its own maiden flight. These two photographs show that a number of no doubt important persons had been invited for the occasion. After a period of testing and further sorrow from an untried engine, a substantial order was placed and the type was officially named Dragon. Although some 200 were built (by Sopwiths), the Dragon became one more aircraft which never entered squadron service in the overcrowded aviation world of late 1918.

Amidst all the feverish activity, Harry Hawker still found time to indulge his other passion – fast cars. He is standing here beside his 225hp Mercedes, while behind him stands the new factory at Ham, built to accommodate the greatly expanded production demands generated by the air war.

The sawmill at Ham.

The 3F.2 Buffalo was originally intended as another 'trench fighter', with the same Bentley rotary as the Salamander, but was, unlike the latter, a two-seater. It first flew in September 1918 and, almost inevitably, also became a victim of the Armistice, with only two being built.

The Buffalo is on the right. The Scarff ring fitted to the gunner's cockpit suggests that it is the second aircraft, H5893. The 'Dragon', on the left, is in fact the second Snipe to be converted to Dragon standard for experimental purposes.

75

One is tempted to imagine a scene one day in 1918 when the busy minds at Kingston looked at one another and the realisation came to them that amid all the aircraft bearing the Sopwith name, not a single monoplane was to be found! At any rate, a Camel fuselage was procured, a parasol wing was fixed on top, the result was christened the Scooter, and Harry Hawker had another aerobatic and general communications aircraft.

In due course the Scooter was glimpsed by the powers-that-be, so they wanted one too. A similar aircraft was ordered for experimental work with possible application as a fighter, and was given the name of Swallow. It went no further, but thus it came about that on the day Sopwiths was wound up, these two aircraft remained the only monoplanes the company had ever produced.

76

Four
Sopwiths in Service

Considering the renown which aircraft bearing the name of Sopwith achieved during the First World War, it is intriguing to contemplate the curious fact that when the Royal Flying Corps first flew across the Channel to battle on 13 August 1914, the squadrons involved (Nos 2, 3, 4 and 5) contained not a single Sopwith machine. However, this simple fact scarcely reveals the whole story, since both the Army and the Navy had numbers of Sopwiths on charge and Kingston products of various kinds were soon in action over both land and sea. As the war years went by, military aviation was destined to undergo changes of great magnitude and scope. By the Armistice, aircraft such as the Sopwith Snipe and Handley-Page O/400 were in service, contrasting greatly with the frail and underpowered Bleriots and Maurice Farmans which first rose to confront the enemy in the skies of 1914. By that time, too, the young Royal Air Force's Order of Battle amounted to well over 200 squadrons, of which there were over thirty squadrons of Sopwith fighters, mostly Camels. At sea, more Camels, together with Cuckoos, were embarked in His Majesty's warships, which by then included the first real aircraft carrier. Other Sopwith aeroplanes had found their way to various corners of the world, some borne on the winds of conflict, others equipping the air forces of countries which, prior to 1914, had scarcely even seen a flying machine.

Although no Tabloids featured in those first gallant formations which flew out from Dover to Amiens in August 1914, several, like the one above, were dispatched to France in packing cases, assembled on the spot and soon flying reconnaissance missions above the battlefields.

One of a motley collection of aircraft impressed into service by the war machine in August 1914 was a second example of the Sopwith seaplane which had so nearly won the Circuit of Britain the previous summer. It was taken on charge by the RNAS and given the service number 151.

An RNAS Schneider being hoisted aboard a naval warship. The sea is calm; in rougher conditions the dainty Schneiders were too often apt to suffer damaged floats.

The Isle of Man steamer *Ben-My-Chree* was also called to the colours, as the RNAS perceived the value of embarking some of its aircraft in specially adapted vessels accompanying the Fleet. Above: a Schneider on board the *Ben-my-Chree* on 3 September 1915, during the Gallipoli episode. Below: a Type 860 seaplane, seen from the deck of the *Ben-my-Chree*. The latter vessel was destined never to see the Isle of Man again. She met her end on 9 January 1917, destroyed in the harbour of Castelorizo Island by Turkish artillery based on the mainland.

Sopwiths travelled even further afield, to another theatre of war, East Africa. This Type 807 is being manhandled across the desert, hopefully to a reunion with its wings and engine.

Two Type 807s were sent to East Africa, where, as well as a land campaign, efforts were directed at finding and destroying the German cruiser. This was eventually successful, but by that time the underpowered 807s had been withdrawn and replaced.

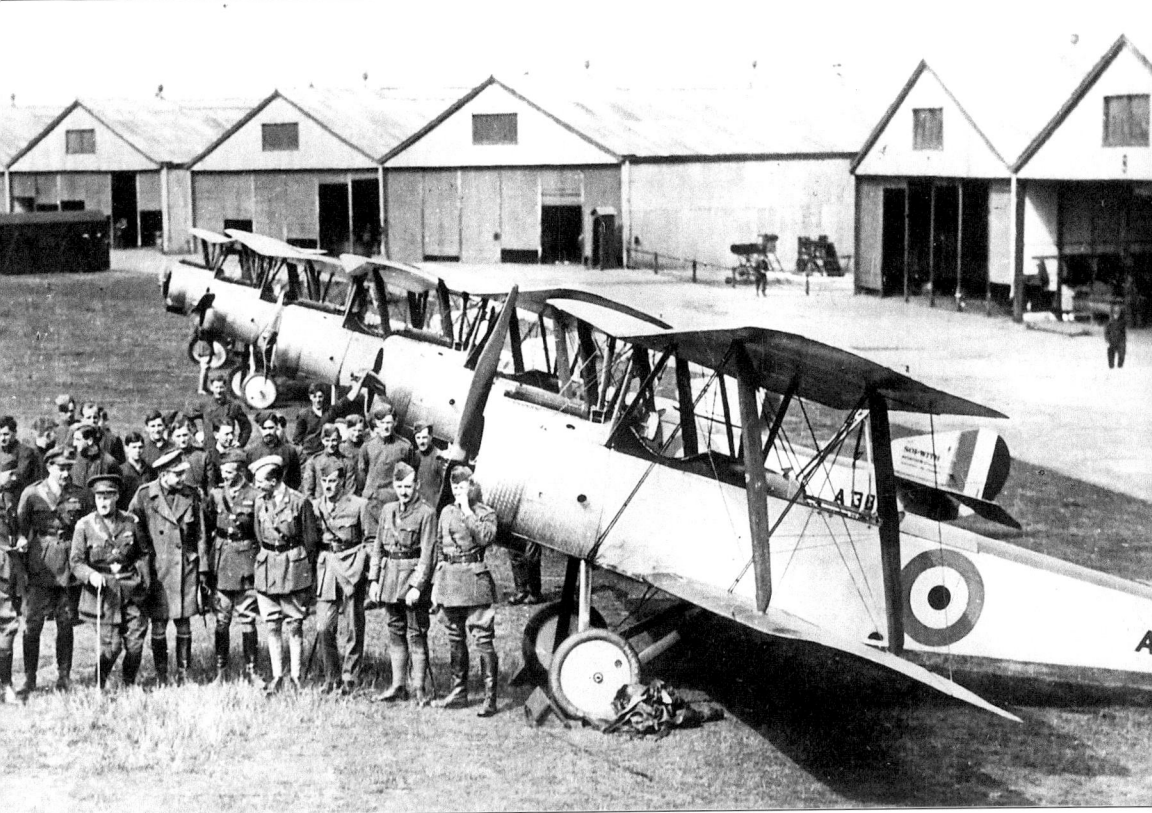

Back in England in May 1916, 'A' and 'B' Flights of 70 Squadron were the first to re-equip with the 1½ Strutter as aircraft became available. Here, 'B' Flight's aircraft are lined up, with their air and ground crew, before departure for the Western Front on 29 June. Fourth from the left in the greatcoat is Captain B.C. Hucks, the famous pre-war aerobatic pilot. 'A' Flight had already left the month before, while 'C' completed the Squadron's deployment at the end of July. On 1 July, 70's Strutters were in the air as, below them on a wide front, the troops on the ground were scrambling out of their trenches to begin the bloody Battle of the Somme.

A snow scene at RNAS Coudequerque, during the severe winter of 1916-1917. If it was cold at airfield level, conditions in a Strutter's open cockpit at 15,000 feet during a two-hour patrol were Arctic.

Another RNAS Strutter in balmier days – at Mullion on 11 June 1917. An unfortunate feature of this type, the undue separation of the two cockpits, impairing communication in flight, is well illustrated here.

Some 4,000 1½ Strutters were manufactured under licence in France and served with the French Aviation Militaire. This one was photographed at Le Crotoy, in 1917, with a Caudron G IV just behind.

Some of 50 Squadron's Camels in their hangar.

No. 4 Squadron of the Australian Flying Corps, being inspected by King George V. A Camel is in the background.

On a misty morning in April 1918, an offensive patrol of Camel F.1s of 209 Squadron RAF, led by Captain Roy Brown DSC, encountered a flight of enemy triplanes led by the redoubtable Manfred von Richthofen. As the formations broke up into separate dogfights, Lt Wilfred May found himself flying for his life along the Somme valley, pursued by the 'Red Baron' in his notorious red triplane. Luck was on Lt May's side. He escaped the fate of the German ace's eighty previous victims, while it was his would-be conqueror himself who fell to his death on the hillside above the river. Capt. Brown (pictured here), having pursued the German in his turn, was credited with a famous victory. Later investigations have tended strongly to support the claims of Australian machine-gunners on the ground to have been responsible for the single bullet through the heart which removed from the scene the most famous, most feared and most successful German air fighter of the war. We shall probably never be sure.

Some Camels came to grief.

Some Camels were captured…

...like this one of Sub-Lieutenant K.D. Campell. He became a POW on 10 March 1918 after being shot down by ground fire.

This Camel, from 208 Squadron, appears to have come down not so very far from the lines. The passers-by – particularly the soldier loitering with his bicycle – seem remarkably unconcerned that the aircraft still has a bomb slung underneath!

A Dolphin with some of its attendant AMs (air mechanics).

A less-fortunate Dolphin, of 'C' Flight, 23 Squadron, after crashing at St Omer on take-off on 3 May 1918. One SE5a pilot, on encountering a Dolphin over that same St Omer, thought he would have a bit of fun in a mock dog-fight with this rather portly aeroplane, but discovered to his chagrin that he was comprehensively out-manouvered.

These Camels of 'A' Flight, No. 9 (N) Squadron were photographed at Leffrinhoucke aerodrome near Dunkirk. The face adorning the fins of four of them is that of the famous comedian, George Robey. The reason for this non-regulation marking is unknown, but one is tempted to imagine that the Flight Commander, on leave in London, saw Robey, then appearing in the 'Bing Boys' shows, was greatly impressed and decided that the Hun should also share in the fun.

Lts Purdey and Daniel, of 43 Squadron.

Capt. J.L. Trollope, a 43 Squadron flight commander, with his 'bus'. On 24 March 1918, in the course of several engagements, he shot down six enemy aircraft in the day.

43 Squadron were flying high. Less than three weeks later, on 12 April, Capt. H.W. Woollett (above) repeated Trollope's feat with a total of fourteen victories for the squadron in the day – a new record. Although air fighting still claimed many lives, the Royal Air Force was gradually gaining ascendancy over the Imperial German Air Service, thanks partly to machines like the Sopwith Camel.

The Camels of 'C' Flight, 10 (N) Squadron.

A Pup of 4 (N) Squadron, at Bray Dunes, also just outside Dunkirk.

The pilots of 65 Squadron with one of their Camels at Wyton, Huntingdonshire, in September 1917.

80 Squadron, equipped with Camels, was formed at Montrose on 1 August 1917. In November, it moved to Beverley, East Yorkshire, landing on the racecourse, where this picture was taken. From left to right, standing: Lts Welch, Bennett, Oldridge, Brown, Maj. Bell, Capts Hall, Whistler, Lts Gardner, Preston. Seated: Lts Chadwick, Murray, Milligan, Holt, Potter. The Squadron flew to Boisdinghem in France on 22 January 1918.

When Zeppelin raids on London first started in 1915, the resources available for airborne defence against them were meagre. One method which was tried involved fitting Pups with Le Prieur rockets. This Pup was photographed at Eastchurch on 25 October 1916.

Another Home Defence Pup, showing the slots formed in the upper engine cowling, for cylinder head cooling. In attendance: Capt. Newton and Lt Davies.

Later in the war, it became possible to spare front line aircraft from the Western Front, to combat not only Zeppelins but also the Gotha bombers which superseded them. These Camels of 'C' Flight, 44 (HD) Squadron were based at Hainault Farm. The F.1 'HD' (Home Defence) Camels were specially modified, with the cockpit moved rearwards and the top wing cut-out enlarged in order to improve visibility for night-fighting.

A close-up of the HD Camel cockpit, showing the added head fairing and the two Lewis guns, which replaced the standard Vickers installation for this special work.

After the Austrian victory over the Italians at Caporetto, British and French land forces were sent to Italy in late 1917 to assist in stabilising the situation, accompanied by a RFC brigade, included in which was 28 Squadron, whose Camels are pictured on the airfield at Verona.

No. 226 was another Camel squadron which accompanied the British force to Italy.

The Salonika front, on the northern shores of the Aegean, was a result of the habitually tortuous politics of that region, made more so by the interventions of the major belligerent nations. The Allies wanted Greece on their side, the Central Powers wanted Turkey. Greece wanted to expand eastwards at Turkey's expense, while, just to the north lay Serbia, the start of all the trouble, but defeated and overrun by the Austrians in late 1915. Constituting other pawns in the game, were Rumania and Bulgaria. To the north-east loomed the Russian bear. These $1\frac{1}{2}$ Strutters belong to 'F' Squadron RNAS, based at Stavros, one of the Aegean island bases used by the British. The date is 29 April 1917.

The RNAS base at Aliki Bay, on the island of Imbros, a few miles to the westward of Gallipoli, was established in 1915. Tabloid 1202 stands parked, with the Officers' Mess just behind.

This 1½ Strutter was brought down at Radulevo by Corporal Ahlen in a Halberstadt. The crew, Lts Brady and Marsh, were wounded.

Lt Jack Alcock, later to achieve undying fame by his transatlantic flight in 1919, with his triplane at Stavros.

Major William Barker VC, a Canadian, commanded 139 Squadron, flying Bristol fighters, but preferred the Camel above for his own use.

Lt Col. S.E. 'Crasher' Smith also chose a Camel as his personal aircraft, seen here at Aulnoy, with a DH 9A of 99 Squadron behind.

Various means were tried to operate aircraft, other than seaplanes, successfully from the Navy's warships. This Baby was fitted with skids, the idea being that they should run along guides, to eliminate a problem then perceived of the aircraft swinging during take-off.

This 1½ Strutter went one further: as well as the skids, flotation bags were fitted to keep the aircraft afloat after ditching and while awaiting recovery.

A defining moment in the evolution of naval aviation: On 2 August 1917, Squadron Commander E.H. Dunning, in a Pup, achieved the first landing on a ship – the partially converted ex-battle cruiser HMS *Furious*. This involved an approach through the turbulence created by the midship's superstructure, before straightening up to touch down on the forward flight deck. The two successful landings accomplished represent not only a tribute to the skill and bravery of the pilot, but also probably to the tractability of the Pup. Five days later, on a third attempt, the aircraft went over the side and Dunning was killed.

The wreckage of Dunning's Pup being recovered.

Lighters were another solution that was tried. The lighter, equipped with a wide wooden flight deck, a Camel and its handling party, was towed at speed behind a destroyer …

…this provided a satisfactory 'wind over the deck' and an exciting time was had by all. On 11 August 1918 off Heligoland, Lt S.D. Culley was launched in this manner in a Camel 2F.1 and shot Zeppelin L53 down in flames. Returning to the mother destroyer, Culley ditched successfully and was picked up. To set the seal on a successful operation, the aircraft was also recovered and even survives to this day in the Imperial War Museum.

Camels ranged on the forward flight deck of HMS *Furious*. On 19 July 1918, the first carrier-borne raid in the world was launched against the Zeppelin hangars at Tondern in the far north of Germany (now in Denmark). Seven Camels were dispatched from *Furious* which, accompanied by a protective cruiser screen, had steamed to within range of the target. The raid was counted a success, two Zeppelins being destroyed. It was, however, a success bought at a price. Since Dunning's brave experiments, *Furious* still retained its obstructive midship's superstructure and landing back on the parent vessel was not yet considered operationally feasible. Aircraft, once launched, were therefore still required to ditch alongside, with the pilot hopefully being hauled back on board, but leaving the aircraft likely to be a total loss. In the event, four Camels were obliged to divert to neutral Denmark and internment, while the others ditched in the sea, with the loss of one pilot. Nevertheless, the operation marked the arrival of the aircraft carrier as an essential component of any modern fleet. Twenty-two years later, still flying biplanes, the Royal Navy launched its celebrated attack on the Italian fleet in Taranto harbour. Later on, in the Pacific war, the Battle of Midway confirmed the aircraft carrier as the fleet's new capital ship. Many years later still, the ghosts of Tondern were surely watching with approval when, in the waters around the Falkland Isles, the only in-theatre aerial strike force and fighter cover available to the South Atlantic Task Force was provided by the Sopwith Camel's direct lineal descendents – the Harriers embarked in HMS *Hermes* and HMS *Invincible*.

Snipes of No. 1 Squadron over Baghdad, at a time when the appearance of RAF fighters over that city could take place perfectly serenely, with no fear of the vigorous and lethal protest from the ground it would be greeted with today!

Swinging the propeller on a Dolphin of 79 Squadron, which in February 1919, based at Bickendorf, Cologne, was part of the 'Watch on the Rhine'.

Flt Lt C.A. Stevens MC in a Snipe at the fourth RAF Pageant, held at RAF Halton in June 1923. Snipes remained in service with the RAF until 1926.

A landplane version of the Baby belonging to the Norwegian Air Force. Baby seaplanes were supplied to Norway in 1917.

These three 2F.1 Camels had been supplied to the Latvian Air Force in 1919. This photograph was taken at Riga on 4 August 1921.

Camels of the Finnish Air Force being inspected by the President of Finland.

Five
Atlantic Failure

In 1913, Lord Northcliffe, proprietor of the Daily Mail and great benefactor of British aviation, offered a prize of £10,000 for the first successful non-stop crossing of the Atlantic Ocean, from any point in North America to a landing in Europe. At that stage in its development, aviation was scarcely in a position to respond to the challenge, with the flimsy airframes and unreliable engines then at its disposal. In any case, circumstances soon demanded that any such projects be laid aside, in favour of the prosecution of the 'Great War'. When at last the guns fell silent, the project had been placed firmly in the realm of the possible by the technical advances engendered by the fires of war. In a number of quarters, no time was lost in returning to it. Inevitably, Sopwith were not to be excluded from such a company and a version of the B.1 bomber was produced in which Harry Hawker, with his chosen navigator Kenneth Mackenzie Grieve, proposed to make the attempt. They did not lack competition. The Sopwith team arrived in Newfoundland with their machine on 28 March. A fortnight later they were joined by another entry, in the shape of Fred Raynham, with his navigator Morgan and their Martinsyde aircraft, while other teams, notably those organised by Vickers and Handley-Page, were on their way. In the event, the first men to succeed in flying across the Atlantic were Cdr Read USN and his crew in the American Curtiss flying boat NC-4, who took off from Trepassey Bay on 16 May and landed on the Tagus, at Lisbon, on 27 May. The lapse of eleven days was due to a protracted stopover in the Azores. Since the flight was not non-stop, this meant not only that they were ineligible for the Daily Mail prize, but also that their feat, although considerable, lacked, in the public's eyes at least, the drama and significance with which the subsequent direct attempts were imbued.

The Atlantic. Once in Newfoundland, the four-bladed propeller was discarded in favour of one with two blades, with a view to achieving an improved take-off performance. The small airscrew on the fuselage side drove the wireless generator, but, in fact, one was not carried on the attempted crossing.

Before departure from England, a number of test flights were made, including one of nine hours (above). On 20 March 1919, Hawker and Grieve sailed from Great Britain in the *Digby*, bound for Newfoundland and accompanied by the Atlantic, dismantled in two large packing cases. For the time being, however, it was the Newfoundland weather which was to control events. To begin with, St Johns at that time of year was still ice-bound, so that the *Digby* was obliged to anchor in Placentia Bay, to the south-west, where the aeroplane, still in its packing cases, was transferred to another vessel, the *Portia*. Hawker and Grieve proceeded to St Johns by rail, leaving the Atlantic to follow by sea when conditions were suitable. At St Johns, they were soon joined by Raynham and Morgan, and the two flight crews settled in at the Cochrane Hotel, in a friendly but wary brotherhood, watching both the unco-operative weather and one another.

The Atlantic being transferred from the *Digby* to the *Portia* in Placentia Bay.

Once the weather allowed it to be landed at St Johns, the aeroplane had another six difficult miles to cover overland, to reach the small, muddy, L-shaped area which had been chosen for the take-off. Horsepower was the only means available.

From The Battery, on the outskirts of St Johns, the *Portia* is seen steaming into the harbour, complete with its deck cargo. Through April and into May, the weather still held centre-stage, preventing departure and causing frustration to the four aviators. On 10 May, the three American flying boats began to arrive in Trepassey Bay. Simultaneously, the weather started to pick up. In the evening of Friday 16 May, the big flying boats departed and set course for the Azores. The game was afoot: when he heard the news, Hawker lost little time in making his decision. In the afternoon of 18 May, the Atlantic slowly accelerated across the primitive airstrip and lumbered into the air. Slowly, it gained height and disappeared eastwards over the misty ocean. No more was heard of it and its two crew on that day, nor during the days that followed. No drone of engine, no speck in the western skies, no lone aircraft landing in triumph on the shore of Ireland. As the days passed, the nation was obliged to conclude that it had two more heroes to mourn, so soon after the ending of the war that had taken so many. Hawker's presumed widow received a letter of condolence from the King. It was 25 May before a small Danish cargo vessel, the *Mary*, sailing by the Butt of Lewis, signalled that she had the two aviators on board, safe and sound, having plucked them from the sea days before. The world was to learn that, when they were well on their way across the ocean, the engine water temperature had started to rise; despite all that Hawker tried, it had remained so, finally reaching boiling point. In the end, the only choice left was to seek a ship alongside which they could ditch. In heavy seas, the *Mary's* whaler brought them on board. However, the little ship was one of those that had still not been equipped with a radio and thus had been dumb until it could be in visual contact with the shore. Once the news was passed, a destroyer was dispatched to meet her and the two fliers began to make their way back to London and a tumultuous reception.

Meanwhile, the wreckage of the Atlantic was still afloat, having been abandoned when its crew was rescued. By chance, it was sighted by another passing vessel, the *Lake Charlotteville*, which took it on board.

The wrecked aircraft was brought ashore at Falmouth, whence it was conveyed to London and exhibited on the roof of Selfridges in Oxford Street.

The crowd at Kings Cross to greet the arrival of Hawker and Grieve, including many Australian soldiers who had not yet returned home after the end of the war. It is difficult to imagine such a scene taking place today. It reflects, on the one hand, the fame which, in those early days of flying, generally attended the activities of the pioneer aviators and Harry Hawker in particular and, on the other, the dramatic circumstances of the pair's disappearance and their almost miraculous return. Although they had failed to win the *Daily Mail*'s £10,000, the newspaper, in recognition of their gallant exploit, generously awarded them a consolation prize of £5,000. From the authorities, they each received the Air Force Cross.

From left to right: Mackenzie Grieve, Sopwith, Mrs Muriel Hawker, Harry Hawker.

Just under four weeks later, Jack Alcock and Arthur Whitten Brown, in their twin-engined Vickers Vimy, took off from Munday's Pond near St Johns (above) and set out eastwards in their turn, through the grey inhospitable skies above the North Atlantic. Sixteen hours later, they made landfall in western Ireland. Theirs was the success which might so easily have been Hawker's and Grieve's.

113

Passengers of the modern jet age, conveyed in your thousands to and fro across that same Atlantic in your airborne armchairs, cosseted by stewardesses, comforted by air-conditioning, fortified by the occasional consoling glass and beguiled by in-flight entertainments, never forget the debt you owe to those few pioneers whose courage and fortitude blazed the trail you now follow in such ease and comfort. Remember that they flew the same skies as you, at lower altitudes amid the turbulent clouds and frozen in their open cockpits, cut off from the world in the bleak Atlantic night, with little more than a wayward magnetic compass as guide – no radio-navigational aids or inertial platforms for them. Remember and salute them!

Six
The End – and the Beginning

It was a very different company which returned to the ways of peace from that little band who faced the challenge that arose in August 1914. Unfortunately, the extensive organisation and large production capacity which, under Tommy Sopwith's leadership, had been built up during the war years, had now to be drastically slimmed down. At the same time, projects had still to be devised and made and, hopefully, sold, in order that profits could still pay the shareholders' dividends and to fill the pay packets of the workforce that remained. At the same time, Sopwith and his associates were not the men to ignore new challenges like the Atlantic crossing and the revived Schneider Trophy. However, in the end, the battle was lost through lack of adequate orders and the company was wound up. The knock-out blow came from a government which, having recently demanded maximum output, suddenly discovered some hefty tax demands, apparently associated with the contracts it had placed and urged on the company in time of war. Out of these financial ashes there was to grow, almost immediately, the new company of H.G. Hawker Engineering Limited, still directed by Tom Sopwith, but named after the young Australian who had contributed so much to the success of its predecessor. Although, within a year, Harry Hawker was to be killed in a flying accident, his name lived on, as the new company survived the difficult early years and gradually thrived to produce, first the Hart and all its variants and then, as the Second World War beckoned, the immortal Hawker Hurricane.

The great assembly hall at Ham. Lines of half-finished Snipes and Salamanders fill one bay, but, symbolically, little activity is to be seen. The echoing silence can be imagined.

Just one bay of the great hangar contains upwards of sixty aircraft. These will probably be delivered but, already, the dread obituary 'surplus to establishment' was waiting to bring their lives to a premature end, particularly in the case of the Salamanders. As Versailles converted the Armistice into a permanent peace, the RAF was rapidly pared down, all but 33 of the 263 squadrons it possessed when the fighting stopped being disbanded. Well, at least the RAF was still flying Snipes. Surely, it would soon need newer, more advanced machines, as aviation technology continued to advance? For the time being though, the political trend was very much in the opposite direction. In time, the RAF would grow again and in time the squadrons would be re-formed, not least through the efforts of Tommy Sopwith's one-time pupil, now Air Marshal Trenchard and Chief of the Air Staff, but for now that time still lay in the future.

On 4 December 1918, matters were not helped by a power cut. A traction engine was enlisted to drive the shaft for the workshop machines.

One product that was adopted to swell the order books to replace the missing aircraft contracts was saucepans. Another was motor cycles. (One may without difficulty guess which was the more popular with men more used to producing high-speed fighters – indeed, the influence of Harry Hawker himself may be sensed here).

117

The motor cycles were exhibited at Olympia, as this fleet of vans proclaims.

Aircraft were, of course, still the real business of Sopwith. Another triplane, the Cobham, was a bomber – a three-seater this time – whose principal claim to fame lies in the fact that it was the one and only Sopwith type which was not single-engined. Only two were built, the Mk I and the Mk II. Just to aid confusion, it was the latter, powered by Siddeley Pumas and seen above, which flew first, in mid-1919, some nine months before the Mk I – it was delayed by the non-availability of its own intended engines, the ever-recalcitrant ABC Dragonfly.

The Snark (above), like the Cobham, had its genesis in early 1918, though it too did not take the air until the following year. Apart from its biplane configuration, the Snapper (below) could be called a sister to the Snark, being designed to the same specification and sharing, with the Cobham Mk I, the same 360hp ABC Dragonfly (shades of the Pup's 80hp, only two or three years earlier!). Only three of each type were built.

With the ending of the war, thoughts naturally once more turned to the peaceful uses of aeroplanes. The Dove was derived from the Pup and, indeed, used the same engine. It was intended as a light sports aircraft, no doubt aimed at the many young men who had been taught to fly at the Nation's expense and had discovered great pleasure in chasing through this newly-discovered world above and between the clouds. Unfortunately, these young men now found that the Nation was no longer keen either to pay them or to supply them with an aircraft for that purpose, and alas, most of them found that their pockets did not match their dreams.

A single-seat version of the Dove in flight. Some ten Doves were made and sold, but it was trying to occupy a position which really only came into existence a few years later, then to be memorably filled by the de Havilland Moth.

120

The Gnu was another attempt to enter the civil field, with an enclosed cabin for two passengers behind the pilot. The vision would have been of a machine which could be used for giving 'joy-rides' to fare-paying members of a public, overwhelming numbers of which had in those days never left the ground.

Harry Hawker entering a Gnu, showing the cabin cover hinged back. Around a dozen Gnus were made – not enough to provide a commercial success. This aircraft also used a rotary, mainly the 110hp Le Rhône. Such engines had proved their worth in the recent conflicts, but were less than ideally suited to private ownership and a Sunday afternoon pleasure 'flip'.

As the Peace Conference convened in Paris, the British people, with relief, returned to their habitual pursuits: the Grand National took place at Aintree on 28 March, in May the County Championship was resumed while, in September, the Schneider Trophy contest was scheduled to be held, at Bournemouth. For their entry, Sopwith designed and built a special machine, in which was fitted a 450hp Cosmos Jupiter, designed by Roy Fedden (Cosmos then having yet to be absorbed by the Bristol Aeroplane Company). In trials, an encouraging 180mph was recorded. However, on the day of the contest itself, nothing much went right: both the Supermarine and the Sopwith entries were damaged and retired; fog then spread over the course and the race was abandoned for that year.

The 'Schneider', as it was inevitably dubbed, with attendant fitters.

After the Schneider Trophy debacle, the aircraft was converted to a landplane, renamed the 'Rainbow' and re-engined – with another example of that troublesome type, the Dragonfly. It took part in the 1920 Aerial Derby, but was disqualified when Hawker failed to finish correctly. Reunited with its Jupiter, it was entered for the 1920 Gordon Bennett contest, but was withdrawn when Sopwiths was liquidated.

Coming events cast their shadow before. The Rainbow resurfaced in 1923, coming second in that year's Aerial Derby, when the old name took equal place with the new.

The solitary Grasshopper to be made had a 100hp Anzani radial engine and was another one aimed, unsuccessfully, at the then exiguous light aeroplane market.

The Wallaby not only resembled the Atlantic structurally (although it had three-bay wings) and, like the latter, used a Rolls-Royce Eagle VIII, it also was specially produced for a pioneering competition, namely the £10,000 prize offered by the Australian Government in 1919 for the first flight, by Australians, from the UK to Australia. The attempt came to grief in Persia and a Sopwith machine once more found itself beaten by a Vickers Vimy, this time in the hands of Ross and Keith Smith.

Out of the Wallaby came the Antelope, another small commercial aircraft with, like the Gnu, a relatively comfortable and spacious cabin for two passengers behind the pilot's open cockpit. The engine was a water-cooled 200hp Wolseley Viper. Just visible in the photograph is the unusual four-wheeled undercarriage.

125

The 1920 Olympia exhibition, with the Antelope flanked by a Dove and a Gnu. The Antelope appears to be fitted with its original undercarriage, the forward wheels being added later.

126

And what of Sir Thomas (as he was created in 1953)? He was to lead Hawkers and later the great Hawker-Siddeley Group for over forty years, before finally retiring at the age of seventy-five in 1963. If aviation contained his life's work, the sea was often the scene of his leisure hours. He owned a series of ocean-going yachts and twice competed for the America's Cup on behalf of Great Britain, at the helm of *Endeavour* in 1934, and *Endeavour II* in 1937. Above, he is manning the wheel of the former vessel, complete with pipe and the engrossed help of his second wife, Phyllis.

Sir Thomas celebrated his hundredth birthday at his home, Compton Manor, on 18 January 1988 and died, after as full and fulfilled a life as anyone could wish, on 27 January of the following year. Alongside Lady Phyllis, he is buried in the churchyard of All Saints, Little Somborne, Hampshire, the simplicity of their gravestones seeming to typify the unassuming nature of one who was a leading member of that company of great men who drove British aviation forward in its formative years. Some years before, R.J. Ashfield had written of him: 'Mr Sopwith was always a joy to work for, giving praise for a good job and not mincing words over a bad one'.

Selected Bibliography

Blackmore, L.K.: *Hawker*. (Airlife)
Bramson, Alan: *Pure Luck*. (Patrick Stephens)
Brett, R. Dallas: *History of British Aviation, 1908-1914*. (The Aviation Book Club)
Hawker, H.G. and Mackenzie Grieve, K.: *Our Atlantic Attempt*. (Methuen)
King, H.F.: *Sopwith Aircraft*. (Putnam)
Robertson, Bruce: *Sopwith – The Man and his Aircraft*. (Air Review Limited)

Acknowledgements

When, in 1910, Tommy Sopwith wanted to begin his flying career, where should he go but to that Mecca for modern young men, Brooklands in Surrey? It was thus fitting that I should begin my researches for this book there, in the Archive Library of the Brooklands Museum. A significant proportion of the photographs in this book are from those Brooklands records and I should like to express my grateful thanks to Julian Temple and Mike Goodall, for their courtesy and for permission to use them. I obtained a considerable number of photographs from the J.M. Bruce/G.S. Leslie collection and I should like to thank Stuart Leslie for his generosity and help. A third source which I was able to tap was the collection of the late A.E. (Bert) Tagg, whom I am glad to have known.

A number of photographs were obtained from the Library of the Royal Aeronautical Society, which has kindly agreed to their publication. My thanks go also to Terry C. Treadwell, for lending me some fine examples of his own collection, and in particular to Mrs Joan Oram, whose father, Stanley Witt, was engaged in building Sopwith fighters in 1918 (he can be seen, standing third from the right, in the lower photograph on page 64). Acknowledgements are also due to Bruce Robertson, R. Sturtivant and W. Jacobs (via Stuart Leslie). Torquay Library and the Museum of Army Flying, Middle Wallop, also supplied two of the photographs.

In addition to the above, for their help, I should like to express my gratitude to, firstly, Derek James, for the loan of some of the relevant literature, Mr R.J. Varney (whose father Len Varney, served as an engine fitter in the Royal Flying Corps), Tom Griffiths, H.W. Foot of the Museum of Army Flying, the staff of the Kingston Heritage Centre and, lastly, Reg Payne, a life-long Hawker man.